Jacky Newcomb is the UK's leading expert on the after-life, having dedicated her life to the subject. She is a *Sunday Times* bestselling author with numerous awards to her name, a regular columnist for *Take a Break*'s *Fate & Fortune* magazine, and is a regular on ITV's *This Morning*, Lorraine Kelly's show and C5's *Live with Gabby*.

Also by Jacky Newcomb:

Touching Heaven

Touching Heaven

True stories of spiritual experiences

Jacky Newcomb

Harper
True *Fate*

A few details have been changed to protect the privacy
of the individuals concerned.

HarperTrueFate
An imprint of HarperCollins*Publishers*
1 London Bridge Street
London SE1 9GF

www.harpertrue.com
www.harpercollins.co.uk

First published by HarperTrueFate 2014

A catalogue record of this book is
available from the British Library

ISBN: 978-0-00-810512-9

Chapter 1

Over the Wall

Many years ago, when I was a child, I was lying in the dentist's chair when I had an extraordinary experience. I'd been given gas – nitrous oxide (laughing gas, as it's sometimes called due to the giggles people can get with smaller quantities) – and had been unconscious. I remember being in a tunnel, which was spinning, and various people were travelling through it towards a bright light at the end. I remember most clearly a couple were ballroom dancing towards the light, but others were sitting or standing around the edges of the tunnel. I felt euphoric.

Being in this tube of light was amazing. I wanted to keep travelling towards the light but all of a sudden I could hear my name being called. 'Come on, Jacky, it's all over now. You can wake up …' followed by, 'She doesn't seem to want to wake up. Give her more oxygen.' Then I was back. Mum had been called in from the waiting room to help rouse me and I always wondered: did something go wrong or was this a natural side effect of the gas?

Years later I studied near-death experiences and realised that what I had been through that day was very similar to what people who've been brought back from the very brink of death have described. The tunnel I found myself in seemed just like those I'd read about in others' true-life stories, and I mentioned it briefly in another book I wrote on the subject, *Heaven*. During my research I've discovered that I'm not alone!

During near-death experiences, or NDEs as they are also known, there are many types of phenomenon that people go through. When the physical body 'dies', even momentarily, you'd assume that nothing would be happening to that person – they are dead, after all! Yet nothing could be further from the truth. When all activity stops in the body (no heartbeat, no blood pressure, etc.), the soul continues to exist and begins its own journey. What happens next is astounding, and this is what I'd like to look at with you in this book.

It's true that some people experience nothing during the time of physical death (of those whose heart is started again and come back to tell us, I mean). Yet others experience an out-of-body sensation; they feel their spirit is floating up and away from their physical body, free and detached as a separate entity. Of these, some explain how they immediately become very aware of their surroundings and can hear what is happening around them. It's common, for example, for the recently deceased person to hear their doctor saying, 'We've lost her …' or, 'Pass me the [insert name of life-saving drug or piece of medical equipment]!' Yet the deceased has no special interest in what is going on, often wondering why people are making such a fuss when they themselves feel very much alive.

The soul might consider various questions, like, 'Am I actually dead now, then?' By far the vast majority are not concerned by that. They feel completely at peace and relaxed. Their only worry might be how relatives and friends will react to the notion that they have died, and this can draw them (or their spirit) to their loved ones' side here on earth.

They could, for example, find themselves floating towards a gathering of terrified relatives who are waiting for news at the hospital. They might hear what they are saying or feel their strong fear that someone they care about deeply might die. In some instances, the new spirit finds itself drawn to those who may be unaware of the drama unfolding with their loved one; the spirit is transported spontaneously to people they care about, be it locally or the other side of the world. In this out-of-body state they see relatives at home, work or school, going about their normal routines. Strangely, it's been known for the living to pick up on the spirit and to either see or sense that something is wrong.

If the doctors revive the 'dead' body, the spirit can usually take these experiences back with them. They recall what happened upon waking and stun everyone with their psychic out-of-body adventures. Being able to describe what they saw afterwards in some way proves that these experiences are real. The spirit clearly has left the physical body and separated in some way. If you can tell your friend, 'At ten past three, when I died, I saw you reading the paper in your garden,' and that was exactly what was happening, then you have to assume that the spirit has separated and become distinct from the physical body. In other words, this stuff is real!

This sets up more questions than answers, really, and I remember questioning this phenomenon after having my own out-of-body experiences when I was a young woman (and also as a child). I had a spooky realisation, which went something like this: if my spirit is leaving my body at this moment and the 'real me' is the one that has the consciousness now in this 'spirit body' then it means I am not my body. If I am a spirit, it means I have come from someone before I appeared or took over this physical body. It also means that when my physical body dies, I continue to live and go on, or perhaps go back to somewhere … Heaven, maybe? (You can see why I have dedicated so many years of my life to studying this awesome subject!)

After her physical body died, one woman saw her mother in the waiting room at the hospital and noticed that she was wearing slippers on her feet instead of outdoor shoes. When the doctors managed to get the daughter's heart beating again and she was a little better, she remembered seeing her mum wearing the slippers at the hospital and asked her about it. Her mum was stunned. Her daughter had died, revived and then been unconscious for hours afterwards, so there was no way she could have known this. What happened apparently was that she had rushed to the hospital to be at her seriously ill daughter's bedside and hadn't even had time to put her shoes on. In the rush she had left the house wearing exactly what she had on!

I know other people have seen the 'tunnel' and had various paranormal experiences during dental visits like I did, but whether it was because they were near to death or simply that the gas mimics the phenomenon is hard to tell. When, as a child, my next dental treatment was due I was excited to see the tunnel of light again, but the dentist seemed less keen to administer the gas. As I was so frightened of the treatment we persuaded him to give it another go, but this time my experience was not so good. I still found myself in the tunnel, and the light was still there at the end, and like many near to death I found I wanted to go towards it. Surely going to the light means death, but the light was very seductive and at first I felt the same great sense of peace and one-ness. This time, though, a large monster-like creature was barring the way. It was standing right in front of the light and I found myself desperately trying to pull away from it and get back into my body.

All too soon the familiar calling of my mother's voice brought me out of my stupor, but the excitement of my first experience hadn't been repeated! For some reason my dentist refused to use nitrous oxide on me again ... but you know what? I didn't want it anyway. Had something happened to me physically during my treatment? If it had, they never said. I know they found it less challenging to wake me this second time. Yet in a way I felt tricked by the light. I always felt that the monster was no dream and that someone somewhere had placed the creature in the tunnel to stop me floating too far away from my body.

Many years later, when a teenager, I read the book *Life After Life* by Dr Raymond A. Moody. Dr Moody recorded many experiences of near death and the phenomena people described. It was here that I first read about the tunnel of light seen during near-death experiences, and I compared the incident I'd had as a child. Now I was hooked, and although I was unable to find further reading material at that time, as an adult I picked up the thread and carried on studying. This time, I was the one collecting stories and I was the one writing the books about them.

So many people around the world believe that life ends when the physical body passes away. Over many, many years of research I've investigated literally thousands of stories of our continuing existence and I've made it my mission to share the best of these with you. I select from hundreds and thousands of case studies on file. Some get chosen for the books, and others get rejected not because the phenomenon is any less interesting, but because so many people have similar encounters.

Where do we go when we pass through the light? What happens next? Heidi was one of many who shared her experience with me. She lost her mother about four years ago (at the time she wrote to me). She said it had been a very long journey and life-changing in so many ways. Her mum had been one of the strongest and most amazing women she had ever known. She showed Heidi so much love in life, and apparently this has continued in death.

Heidi explained that a couple of years ago an aunt contacted her. The aunt hadn't been especially close to her mother but she telephoned 'out of the blue' to share a dream with Heidi. The aunt explained that she'd had the dream a couple of weeks earlier but at first had chosen not to say anything about it. She then explained: 'That was until your mum started to bug me every night since.' Heidi's mum had appeared after death, explaining that she wanted a message to be passed along to her daughter.

Heidi's mum was determined that her afterlife contact should be shared with her loved one. She'd tried reaching out to her daughter personally but explained that Heidi 'hadn't been listening'. Heidi believes this was because she was having a difficult time with her mother's death; she was more closed down and most nights would simply cry herself to sleep. Maybe the spirit was unable to get through due to Heidi's grief, or it might have been that she tried to reach out to her daughter when she was asleep (or at a certain time in her sleep cycle) and wasn't able to because when she tried Heidi was restless and awake.

Her aunt confessed that she really did not know why Heidi's mum had chosen to come to her with the message, but she knew she had no choice but to pass it on. Her mum had stated that Heidi kept locking herself in the bathroom and sobbing over the loss of her mother, saying how much she missed her. She had been trying to comfort her daughter, but Heidi herself had not recognised that the spirit of her mother was there by her side. Next in the aunt's dream a light appeared, a light more beautiful than anything she had ever seen in her life. The aunt began to describe the colours she saw and said they were ones she had never seen or known to exist on earth. I've commented previously about the vibrant colours people see during near death or contact with those who have passed over. It is one way that we know this is no ordinary dream!

Heidi could tell by her aunt's voice that this experience had truly touched her. The aunt continued relating her dream by saying that out of the magnificent light she recognised the voice telling her to please let her daughter know that she was okay and that she didn't want her to grieve any more. She wanted Heidi to know that she loved her so much and that she knew she was loved in return. She said she had been trying to pass the message on herself, but the grief was not allowing Heidi to hear her. One day, she explained, they would be together again, and finally she said she wanted Heidi to please be happy.

I love that! What an important message for us all. Wouldn't we want to say the same thing if we were the ones who had passed on? We'd want those who were left behind to live a good life and be happy. Heidi told me, 'I know my aunt felt the same as me – why in the world would my mum come to her in a dream out of everyone she could have chosen? Then it hit me: she came to my aunt because she knew that she was the one person I would never have expected to hear that from.'

One thing I have learnt is that the deceased will reach out to the living if they possibly can. They will try to contact us first of all. Then, if that doesn't work, they will try someone close to us. This contact was especially clever. Given that the relative wasn't particularly close, by their own admission, there was no reason why Heidi's aunt would have made up the message just to comfort her niece. She only passed on the dream visit because it was so clear and powerful she felt she had no choice. It was almost as if the spirit would have visited over and over until her mission had been completed – and actually, it looks like this is exactly what she was doing. Love is a powerful thing. It shows how strong the bond is, even in death. This clever woman wasn't going to let a little thing like death stop her daughter knowing she was loved!

Over the years I've worked with many health-care workers, doctors and nurses. Those who work with the dying and the deceased will tell me how this kind of afterlife contact comforts the living. After death, many spirits stay close to the earth planes, watching their loved ones, trying to comfort them and even witnessing their own funerals. They are barely out of the living world, simply shedding their body and moving into their new plane. The fine fabric of the spirit is (usually) not visible to the human eye, although we often experience their presence.

The spirit seems to be able to manipulate minor things in the world around us: flickering lights, moving things around, bringing scents and small touches. They can interact with us a little, but I imagine it's a frustrating exercise. Imagine putting your arms around someone who can't feel your touch. Imagine speaking to someone who can't hear your words … This is where a dream visit is so helpful. When our own bodies are in an altered state of consciousness (for example, dreaming, meditating, unconscious …), contact can be made more easily between the spirit and our own soul. Once our daily awareness is out of the way it makes it easier for spirits to reach us and communicate. These afterlife interactions bring us a wealth of experience and knowledge about what it's like in the heaven side of life. In this instance the aunt was able to share the small glimpse of it that she'd seen during her dream-visitation contact. In this illustration she was able to see the beautiful light, which is common in many heavenly encounters, and the vibrant and unusual colours.

Heidi's aunt is not the only one, though. Natisha also saw colours during a near-death experience. She told me that when she was twenty-one she had a major car accident; it was, in her own words, very nasty. It was the most traumatic event of her life, but she always maintained a positive attitude. The consequences of the accident were that she had been left with internal bleeding, punctured and collapsed lungs and much more. The doctors had called Natisha's parents to tell them of the accident and had warned them that she was not expected to survive the night. I can't imagine a more shocking thing for a loving parent to hear than that their child is about to die.

That was twenty-five years ago and I'm pleased to say that Natisha is still here. The experience, though, has never been forgotten. At the time of the accident doctors put her in an induced coma and she lay in the intensive-care unit for a long time. Even though she was paralysed and could not move, she felt her arms reaching out to touch her parents. In some way she connected with the warmth of their hands and recalls that they were touching her back in this altered state of consciousness. Although in this case Natisha didn't die, she was unable to open her eyes because of the coma, and yet she was still aware of everything that was going on around her. She recalls hearing the nurses and doctors talking to each other around the bed – they were discussing her and her case.

One night, when Natisha's family was by her side, she remembers trying to explain to her mum about all the rich, pretty colours she could see; it was, she says, as if she was yelling the information. Yet at the same time she was still in the coma. She wanted her mum to experience it too, to see what she could see. She recalls a stream of brightly enhanced lines towering above her, and when she reached an arm out to grab them, they began to jump around.

(People have spoken to me about seeing these same lines during meditation experiences; they describe it as a holographic grid.)

'What happened next was amazing,' she told me. 'I could feel myself turning my head to the left and all of a sudden four angels with bright-white feathered wings just floated by my bedside.' Natisha turned her head to the other side and four more beautiful and awe-inspiring angels floated towards her. They were all smiling and had their hands out in greeting. At this point she told me that she felt like she was in a sauna; the room became very warm and she was overwhelmed with a feeling of love and purity.

Her grandmother had died six years earlier and Natisha told me that they'd been very close. It was at this point that she looked up and saw her grandma standing at the foot of the bed. The woman spoke and said, 'You are all right. It is not your time yet; go back.'

Natisha felt confused. But her grandma wasn't there to take her to heaven as she'd first thought. Natisha explained that she was more than willing to go, but then the woman disappeared and the angels floated away from her.

Next, a movie screen appeared. It had pictures of a secluded beach containing many large boulders and rocks, both big and small. Natisha was confused. What did it mean? Was her grandmother trying to

Jacky Newcomb

tell her she had a long, rocky recovery ahead? Twenty years later, and Natisha has been with her partner for eleven years. That exact beach is right down the end of the street where they live, just one minute away. It was almost as if she had been given a glimpse of the future, even though at the time she didn't understand. All these years later, it proves to her that the vision she had when she was in a coma was not a random, meaningless dream. Her grandma is still around and continues to make appearances from time to time. Natisha says she feels very blessed indeed.

This is another dream experience from Heidi, whom I spoke about earlier. She confided that her mother had been diagnosed with cancer back in 2009 and was getting sicker by the day. She felt so helpless watching the woman who gave birth to her slip away a little more each day. Heidi had been caring for her when, one night, she had an unusual dream. Her husband, their two boys, herself and her mother were all standing on a sort of dock or bridge, staring at a huge wall. The wall had tons of people trying to climb it and get over the top, Heidi recalls. Then she was aware of helping her mother to climb, eventually getting her to the top and over to the other side to be with the other people.

Although Heidi wasn't able to see what was on the other side of the wall, she knew it was her mother's time to be there. Heidi says she wanted to get the rest of her family to join her mother over the wall, but no matter how hard she tried she couldn't manage it.

About a month later Heidi's mum took a turn for the worse and was rushed to the hospital. Every life-saving measure was put into place, but this was barely keeping her alive. The doctors and nurses kept gently suggesting that she unplug the life-saving equipment (which was no longer helping) and let her mother go. After two days she decided it was what she had to do and her mum quietly slipped away.

Later that week, Heidi was showering, getting ready to go out and make funeral arrangements for her mum, when the dream popped into her head once more. It was then that she realised what it had signified. God was preparing her for what she had to do. Part of her role had been to help her mum get to the other side – shown in the dream as getting over the wall. Suddenly it all made sense.

Chapter 2

Journey to Heaven and the New Life of the Spirit

There are thousands and thousands of stories from people who've encountered near death – people who have almost reached the other side or even crossed through the pearly gates of heaven; they've then been sent back because it wasn't 'their time'. Therefore, these people offer us a glimpse of what lies beyond. Their experiences are many and varied, yet countless people who don't know each other and have never discussed their visions with others see the same things or come back with similar tales. Their afterlife stories are fairly universal. If the brain was making up the scenario, how come so many people of wide and varied backgrounds have the same vision?

Cases of near death go back over thousands of years. Experience of near death has been recorded in some of our greatest books: the Bible features instances of it; Plato, the ancient Greek philosopher, covers the subject in his work *The Republic*, as does, of course, the Tibetan Book of the Dead (the religious text about the afterlife and rebirth), among others.

The subject is now being researched by doctors and scientists alike. We know that the phenomena are real; drugs and hallucinations can't fully explain away these things. Numerous books and papers have been written about people's findings (including many of my own). If you want proof then there is plenty. As strange as this may seem at first, there is more than enough proof to show that the soul is separate from the body.

Here are some of the things that I have discovered through my research:

Before or during the death of the physical body
When dying, the person might become aware of spirits gathering around the bed, or if they are suffering from a long-term illness they may chat to dead relatives every day for long periods of time. At first this might seem like hallucination, but you can ask questions and they will answer you with real answers! Sometimes the dying themselves float in and out of their bodies as their time draws closer; in other words, their spirit leaves their physical body for short periods of time (even though they are still alive), sometimes interacting with angels, guides or deceased loved ones. They might personally be aware of this and talk to nurses, doctors or family about what they have experienced. (Sometimes this

phenomenon happens when a person is sick but not dying, too.)

Others may witness the sick person having what appears to be a one-sided conversation with 'no one'; at other times, nurses, doctors or carers may see a visual representation of the visiting spirits. In the final moments, the dying person may gesture to their 'invisible friends' or sit up to chat, even pointing out people (spirits?) or lights that they can see (though others normally can't). This can be especially strange when the person has previously been non-responsive or even in a coma.

When my mother's partner, Brian, was dying he'd been unconscious for several hours as he slipped away; his breathing was getting shallower and shallower. Then, as his daughter arrived to sit with her dad during his final hours, I decided to make a discreet exit. Walking over to his bedside I went to say goodbye. The unconscious man lifted his head, opened his eyes for the first time in several hours, made direct eye contact with me and smiled. I was blown away! He died around an hour later.

The dying person appears to get one last boost of energy – enough for them to reach out, sit up or even speak, even when they haven't been able to for many days, weeks or months. Medical staff have written to me about this occurrence from all over the world.

Sometimes other family members will receive a visit from the spirit of the still-living person.

Although not yet passed over, the spirit is loose within the body as physical death approaches. The spirit might appear in dreams to their loved ones and their aim is to say goodbye. This is particularly common with young children, where a grandparent will warn the youngster that they are 'leaving' by appearing before them in their spirit form. These experiences are often accompanied by symbolism.

The spirit may be holding a suitcase or have a taxi or aeroplane waiting to escort them to heaven. We call these 'saying-goodbye' dreams or 'announcing' dreams. The spirit pronounces their own death or predicts their close death to those they have left behind, showing that even though they have died they continue to exist.

In her book *Opening Heaven's Door*, Patricia Pearson describes how many people know they are about to die, and observes that clued-in hospice staff will recognise the signs. The dying person starts asking about bus timetables or wants their coat, for example. They begin to talk about travel, but they are actually announcing their own departure. She writes about how, on Christmas Day 2006, the soul singer James Brown announced to his manager, 'I'm going away tonight.' He'd been admitted with pneumonia, but his condition wasn't considered life threatening at the time; he passed away as he'd predicted later that day.

We leave our bodies

As the physical, flesh-and-bones body dies, or at the point when the heart stops, our spirit lifts up and away from the body. As a new spirit we are usually completely aware and still conscious, except that the conscious part of the body appears to have stayed with the spirit rather than the physical body. We realise that we are, and always have been, separate from the spirit.

The spirit might be visually looking forward to where they are being drawn (heaven), or might become fascinated with what is going on around them (looking down at their earthly scene). They could be witness to medical staff working on the body below – most likely their dead or dying body. The spirit may be aware of crowds of people standing around them, after a car accident, for example. At this point, time as we know it has no meaning for the spirit; it ceases to exist.

Sometimes the spirit is drawn to visit a living loved one who might be praying, crying or even unaware that a relative is dying or dead. The spirit might be able to pick up on what their living friend is thinking, as well as being aware of what they are doing. When coming back to their body afterwards they might be able to share what they saw (even viewing loved ones in a different country) while they were officially dead.

On occasion the spirit may be able to connect with a living friend or relation. People have told me that they have heard the disembodied voice of a loved one whisper to them, 'I have to go now,' or, 'I'm okay. I will always love you.' Sometimes the spirit can share energy by merging momentarily with a living loved one; the person might report that they felt a cold shiver or experienced some brief form of paranormal phenomenon and felt certain that the loved one had passed. They will note later that the episode coincided with the exact timing of the death, so they felt they 'knew' that the strange experience had been a visit from the loved one – a real encounter with their spirit.

A place of hell?

Over the years, the place we call hell appears from time to time. It's such a rare occurrence that I almost forgot to add it here, but it seems to be a place where some people have found themselves, living the afterlife they expected after what they had done in life. Previous research shows me that hell is a place lacking in light or love (the Godly light I've already spoken about), and an absence or distancing from God (see my book *Heaven*). People might find themselves momentarily in this place because of anger or because they feel they deserve to be there.

After death, the spirit might feel trapped somewhere, lost or see the 'fire and brimstone' place they were taught about in religious instruction. They might hear screaming, see others in anguish or see confused souls milling around. Yet there is always light somewhere, and it's just waiting to be spotted. When people have described this experience they've talked about also seeing a tiny spot of light in the distance, or a being of light (an angelic type) standing nearby, who is trying to lead them out of this place of anger and fear into a lighter, loving space.

Heaven is a place of forgiveness and unconditional love. The worst of the human race is helped and healed. Even as on earth, no one is beyond saving. People who harm others are always souls who have lost their own way in life, and the place of 'hell' seems to be the same. People are 'trapped' in a hell-like space as long as they allow it to happen, or perhaps until they feel they have been punished enough. This is a self-judgement and on the rare occasions when it has come up in the true-life experiences people have shared with me, those spirits have found their way 'home' again (to heaven) in time ('time' being under our control – in other words, we decide when).

Do I believe in hell? After doing a lot of reading for a previous book I have to say that this lost and trapped feeling does befall the occasional spirit after passing. I only add it briefly here for want of being able to offer full disclosure on the subject. A perfectly lovely lady wrote to me once after a near-death situation to share her terrifying hell-like experience – yet thankfully this is not the norm. Expect to see the light as you cross over, know it is there and follow it. Whatever your life path has been up to that point, you will find the brighter space for sure!

My final thoughts on this are that if you feel you deserve to go to a dark place after you die, take a good look at your life and know that it's not too late to change the way you live right now. If you know you've been a bad person or done bad things, you can atone for them now. Don't waste your life worrying about it. Be a better person from now on!

Many people completely change the way they live their lives after having a near-death experience. After seeing the other side and knowing that life is about love they realise they've wasted their time on earth competing with others or trying to prove they are the best at something. We can do that if we want to, but in the big scheme of things it's nowhere near as important as we think it is. Worst of all, we fall out with people and fight in wars. You might have spent many years becoming top of your profession, yet achieving simple acts of kindness and compassion are far more important goals. We each choose our own life path. We decide where we place ourselves in heaven and on earth. We decide if we want to live good, loving lives.

Please don't worry about passed-over loved ones who may have lost their way on earth. Life is a school of learning, it's hard and we all make mistakes, both small and big. Heaven is a place of healing and forgiveness. Remember that 'punishment' is something we seem to decide for ourselves in heaven – no one judges us but ourselves. This phenomenon has formed less than 1 per cent of all the experiences I've read.

Being collected

It is common after the spirit leaves the body to be 'collected'. An escort appears to take the newly dead spirit to the afterlife. The escort might be an angel, a spirit guide or a previously passed-over relative or friend. The spirit is usually excited to welcome the departed home and may talk about how others are waiting for them. This spirit may or may not be seen by others who are around the bedside at the time of death, and may or may not interact with the person before they pass.

My father had three relatives meet him during a near-death experience, but when he finally died for real, several months later, he came back in a dream to me and explained that a different person was there to collect him – this time it was his father, who had died when he was two years old. In both cases it was deceased relatives who had met him, but later his spirit guide had appeared, a man who identified himself as Peter. Dad was able, as many spirits are, to appear to my sister and me and to share his experiences after death, which I've detailed in my book *Call Me When You Get To Heaven*.

The author Dannion Brinkley wrote a whole book, called *Saved by the Light*, about his extra-ordinary near-death experience. He was met by a shimmering being that looked, he said, like a bag full of diamonds emitting a soothing light of love.

Animals in heaven

Over the years I've been sent numerous readers' true-life experiences that have included animals. Animals (already passed-over pets) occasionally greet the recently departed person, or they connect in the heavenly realms shortly after passing on. When Dad visits my family in dream visitations since passing on, he often appears with departed family pets! We can choose to be with these pets once we cross over, and when we make that journey to the other side they will be waiting excitedly to greet us once more.

How we get to heaven

As I mentioned earlier, some people find their spirit in a spinning tunnel (or vortex) or feel they are drawn towards a bright light in the distance. This spinning might indicate the speeding up of the soul's energy in a way that is necessary to exist in our new dimension. Others feel as if their spirit is being carried along in a type of slipstream or energy river, which carries them gently along as if they were on a boat – and they know that wherever they are going is the right place. In the same way that like attracts like on earth, we end up in the perfect place for our soul growth. Some don't go through a tunnel of light, or don't recall it, but find themselves immediately on the other side.

Other representations of heaven pop up from time to time. Earlier in the book, Heidi described a wall, while some people talk about a gate they have to pass through – one friend of mine was the other side of a gate (although the gate was lying down on some sand). Some see a gap in a hedge or a river they have to cross. Dad often visited me from the other side by rowing across a lake or river (but then, he was a keen fisherman, so this may have been a more appealing visual to him!).

Some see their loved ones visit earth by stepping through a doorway (often a bright light is seen behind them to the realms beyond). The deceased always stop the living from crossing through the doorway or boundary onto their side of life. The boundary is nearly always clearly marked. Heaven is for those who have crossed over or those who almost do! At this point people know that the place beyond the light is our heavenly home, our real state of being, and that earth is a place we visit only for a brief time – a type of school.

Occasionally, people who experience near death do cross this barrier. They get a glimpse of the afterlife and then still get the chance to come back to earth (in other words, a chance for their spirit to go back into the body once more so they can continue to live on earth).

In his fascinating book *Life After Life*, Dr Moody recalls numerous stories of near-death experience that detail the moment of crossing. One account describes a feeling of tumbling or falling in darkness; in the distance was a very brilliant light, which grew larger as the man got closer. Another man talks of moving in a vacuum, a feeling of being halfway here and halfway there. A woman shares her story of hearing a majestic type of music as her spirit left her body, and another woman recalls drifting away from her body to the sound of bells tinkling a long way in the distance.

Healing

If someone passes very suddenly or unexpectedly, or they've previously experienced a long illness that has kept them unconscious, then their death may also be unconscious. One minute they are alive and the next they have died. As you can imagine, this causes confusion for the spirit.

There seems to be a provision for this in the spirit world, as people have described waking up in a hospital setting in the afterlife, a place where they are being cared for by others. They are with groups of other souls in nearby 'hospital' beds, people who have also died. They feel peaceful and calm and know they can stay for as long as they want to.

Some have described long periods of time in a healing environment in heaven, maybe in a healing tube or pod. Others have described a healing light or a 'shower' of healing energy. Once again we seem able to stay in this state for as long as we want, or until we 'awaken' knowing we feel ready to take the next step of our heavenly journey. For the bulk of this time our spirit is in a type of unconscious or unaware state, or drifts in and out of awareness. We are healing once we arrive in heaven. Our soul is becoming whole again.

Religious figures, the light and celebrity greeters

We know from many sources that some people expect to be met by God as they die, or to be greeted by other religious figures. There may have been a longing to meet up again with a long-dead idol from their human existence (a pop or movie star, for example). What tends to happen is that initially the experience seems to match up with human expectation. At first, we see what we are expecting to see, even if that is to be greeted at the heavenly gates by the late singer and movie star Elvis Presley (numerous people have seen Elvis; it's true!).

The 'bright light' at the end of the tunnel is full of unconditional love; it seems to be a living, conscious being. Some people at first believe that this is God but later get a sense that there is an even greater being than the one they are met by. There is no judgement, and we are welcomed by whoever or whatever feels familiar or comfortable to us.

Some souls are escorted to heaven by loved ones, but then a guide or angel meets them as they cross over the barrier. There are lots of variations (all of which I've heard of numerous times), and each experience is normal.

Welcome-home party
It's common to be met by people we interacted with in life, especially people we'd long since forgotten and who've been deceased for many years. The common denominator seems to be that their life crossed yours in some meaningful way – mainly positive. You might see a teacher from your nursery years. That teacher made you feel special during a short period of your life and she recalls you fondly. Your connection helped to form your personality and may have affected hers, too. It's right that she should be among the welcome home crowd.

In another example, say, many years earlier you showed kindness to an elderly man by helping him unpack his car. That moment may have been long forgotten by you but never forgotten by him. He, too, wants to meet you and say thank you. Perhaps in another incident you even saved someone's life. It might not have been a dramatic or memorable thing; for example, perhaps you grabbed the back of their jacket just as they were about to step in front of a car. Your instinctive act could have saved that person's life, but at the time neither of you had any idea how important that moment was.

Your welcome-home committee consists of family, friends, teachers, old work colleagues, friends from clubs and sports and people who used to live next door or down the road. Your group might include pets you had as a child or relatives you never met in life. Your party might include souls you've interacted with in other lives, or relatives and friends who want to thank you for things you did for their loved ones on earth. This group might also include angels and spiritual guides who have helped you during your lifetime or will assist you on the heaven side. Each has a vested interest in your wellbeing and cares for you.

Occasionally you'll see someone you were not keen on in life; usually they have volunteered to act a specific way to help you learn a lesson while you were on earth. Their overall actions may well have been in love, even if neither of you were aware of it at the time. If they abused you or hurt you in some way, you don't need to connect with them in the afterlife if you don't want to. Some people want to make the connection for closure, but others ask that the abuser be escorted away. You only need to think it and it happens (so people have told me).

Touching Heaven

What the soul looks like

Souls in heaven might look like lights or wispy clouds, perhaps with a rough head shape and then a fading glowing outline behind. They might have a golden glow about them or a light emanating from their spirit body. Or the spirit might look much like they did on earth, with a normal-looking body that you recognise from your last life together.

When spirits come to visit us on the earth side (in dreams or waking visions, for example), they usually take on a familiar shape, looking either just as they did, as we know and recognise them, or by choosing to take on a younger appearance. People say their deceased loved ones seem to be vibrant or fizzing with energy when they visit.

The soul may elect to look like their 'best self' or their 'dream self'; they look the way they always wanted to look. The curly hair they always disliked may now be straight; the rounded belly they were embarrassed by may now be flat! Their skin will be glowing, their amputated arm may well be back in place and they don't need to wear that set of false teeth or reading glasses any more. One woman told me that her granddad visits her in dreams and that his hearing 'recovered' after he died, meaning that he no longer shouts at her! Her comments made me laugh. Another said that her father visits her in dreams and appears as if he was around the age of forty. She didn't remember him this way in life and said that she is always amazed at how handsome he looks now.

Their clothing might be robe-like, perhaps appearing as a type of gown or ceremonial dress, but mostly they seem to wear their favourite earth clothes. If they were known for wearing a business suit then it's likely this is what they will appear in if they visit you from the afterlife. My dad materialised to my mother after his passing and he was wearing a blue jumper that she loved. If your loved one was happier in a pair of jeans and a leather jacket, it's likely they'll arrive wearing this. They might wear an item of clothing that we liked to see them in (like Dad did for Mum), or maybe they'll wear something you bought them (or its spiritual equivalent). During 'announcing' dreams the spirit might appear wearing the clothing they were buried in, even if you don't know what clothes these were. If you describe them to someone who does know, you'll likely be stunned when you discover that the exact same tie is on the body ready for burial – naturally this is no coincidence and helps to act as the proof we long for that what we are experiencing is real.

Your life flashing before your eyes
One of the first things to occur on the other side is a past-life review. The new recruit witnesses the life they have just lived on earth and everything they did, said and thought while they were here. You see every

interaction you had and with whom. If you helped someone you experience this from their point of view; if you hurt someone you'll see and feel this, too. You discover how your actions helped you to grow and the life lessons you learned. You'll know how you helped others to grow, too. Many who experience near death have this, too – they literally see their lives pass in front of their eyes, as if watching a movie entitled *This Is Your Life*.

Some people witness this past-life review as if it were happening on a big screen in front of them; others talk about reliving the action and maybe being able to engage in it once more. Some talk of being taken to a 'Hall of Records' or 'Akashic Records' ('Akashic' is a Sanskrit word referring to an ethereal space where knowledge of all past deeds is stored) to view the life they have just lived on earth.

This life vision may be seen with your guardian angel or spiritual guide alongside you; sometimes the experience is in front of a group of elders, advanced spiritual beings or wise ones (see Dr Michael Newton's book *Journey of Souls*). They may take part in the viewing process or simply be with you to discuss it afterwards. We get the opportunity to see how we might have done things better while we lived.

When the author Betty J. Eadie had her life review following a near-death experience, she encountered what she called a 'Counsel of Men' (sometimes called 'the wise ones'). They were sitting around a kidney-shaped table and radiated love towards her. She was told she had died prematurely and must return to her body; she still had work to do here on earth. Betty bitterly resisted, she did not want to come back to earth. But Jesus, who was with her throughout, showed her what her life mission was to be, so she reluctantly agreed to come back once they had promised she could return immediately after she had completed her mission on earth. Betty shared her fascinating experiences in her book *Embraced by the Light*.

During near death when the deceased gets to come back and discuss what happened with the living, people say that the life review seems to take place at lightning speed, even if they've already had a long life and therefore had much to see. People witness their recent life at a much faster pace than it happened in real life. Even so, they are able to keep up and sometimes note that the vision might zoom in or focus on important aspects of their life, while speeding past other, less important parts. The bits of our lives that are significant are often surprising to those who are witness to them.

People report feeling 'shame' while reviewing some parts of their life, or great joy and happiness when reliving others. Even writing about this makes me feel ashamed of those times in my life when I've felt sorry for myself even though others have been much worse off than me. No doubt I'll feel cross with myself once the time comes to see my own past-life review, and I'll get to laugh at myself for having an earthly tantrum! Sometimes I do stop what I'm doing and remind myself, 'One day I'll have to watch this again; am I happy with how I am playing my life?' It really makes me think.

Back from heaven

Following near-death experiences, people are profoundly changed as a result of their encounters on the other side. If they recall a heavenly visit (and not everyone does) then it remains strong in the memory, even many years later. Some folk become religious after their spiritual visions, and others who had strong earthly religious beliefs may change religions or give up their religion altogether, choosing a different, more spiritual path. Some get divorced or suddenly marry, considering life as 'too short', and feel more willing to make life choices relating to love and kindness to others. Some make that job change they've always talked about or train for a completely different career; others give up work and take on more volunteer roles.

Most come back unafraid of death, and many wish they hadn't come back to earth at all! Some feel frustrated that the love they felt on the heaven side is way better than the love they have encountered here. Lots of people feel they are sent back to their bodies either by an angel, a spirit or a deceased loved one who tells them it's not their time.

Nurse Dr Penny Sartori collected many accounts in her book *The Wisdom of Near-Death Experiences*. She records how some bring back psychic phenomena following their afterlife visits, with one woman frightened by her new ability to foresee bad things that were going to happen, including knowing when people were going to die. Some have problems when encountering electrical equipment, picking up static, getting electric shocks and so on. Interestingly, I have this type of phenomena myself.

Many cannot wear watches afterwards because they no longer seem to work, and they find they drain the battery on everything from clocks to children's toys. One interesting development is a new ability with telepathy – being able to connect and communicate with others (living or dead) using the mind rather than words. My husband and I have telepathic contact of some sort on most days; it makes us laugh when we realise it's happening.

Author Dannion Brinkley found he had psychic ability after his own near-death experience. He would 'hear' what people were going to say before they spoke, and was even able to talk along with them as if they had practised a mutual conversation. He confesses that this ability helped him negotiate in business later, as he could even understand conversations in foreign languages.

He also developed the ability to gain snippets of information about the lives of people he met, and on one occasion he seemed to go into a type of trance (as witnessed by a friend) as he picked up a scene from the same spot years earlier just by touching a handrail. This ability is called psychometry – picking up recorded information from an inanimate object.

What do we do in heaven?
The short answer seems to be: anything we want! I've been stunned at the many scenarios that have come up in the thousands and thousands of real-life experiences I've read or been told over the years. Here is a quick list of what spirits tell us they do:

- They visit the living.
- They watch over, guide and guard relatives who are left behind, especially young children.
- They learn to become spiritual guides for the living.
- They work in groups, learning how to use healing energies to help other spirits or living humans (caring for newly crossed-over spirits).
- They play with energies.
- They continue their studies (on how to grow the spirit), looking at other lives and seeing how things could be done better.

- They attend classes.
- They get the opportunity to experience things they were unable to do while living (due to bodily limitations or restrictions of money or location).
- They travel and explore.
- They visit other realms and lands.
- They take part in things that you can't do as a human (fly around, for example).
- They help new spirits to cross over.
- They work with young spirits, or babies.
- They connect to and assist animal energies.
- They greet old friends as they arrive in heaven.
- They teach.
- They create or listen to (merge with) music.

In his book *Heaven and Earth*, Anthony Borgia records his afterlife experiences and contact from his late friend, Monsignor Robert Hugh Benson. Monsignor Benson describes a vivid and busy life in heaven, which includes 'reading' and gatherings and get-togethers with friends both previously known to him and new friends he has made in the afterlife. He describes how they build and create things using thought; these newly created structures are as strong as they might be on earth. He says that spirits continue to work, choosing from a multitude of things that align with their interests and abilities. This work consists of service to others on both sides of life. Isn't it fascinating? We clearly don't sit on clouds all day long playing harps, then!

How is life in heaven different to life on earth?
Well, we don't need to eat or drink anything to survive. We are now spiritual energy beings, so life appears to be sustained by the light. Although we don't need houses, books or any of life's physical items, many still have these in the lower 'entry-level' heavenly realms. We can gather around us 'things' that bring us comfort and create homes (real houses) to live in.

As energy beings we don't need to wear clothes, but as spirits initially maintain a human appearance ('wearing' their recently departed bodies as their chosen shape), they tend to also visually create clothing. Some choose to 'wear' items that are familiar to them or that they would have loved to own.

Heaven consists of many layers, and as we progress through (up?) them our appearance changes; it becomes 'cloudy' as it becomes finer in vibration. Clothing is not so helpful when you resemble a ball of light!

Humans who briefly visit these realms describe the most powerful feeling of love and peace, recalling a blissful state of being. We tend to group or be drawn to others who are like ourselves, including those spirits who were known to us on earth. People describe discovering old friends or connecting with earthly celebrities whom they have admired in life; they seem to be drawn to other spirits with similar energies, too.

What does it look like in heaven?
As we've discussed previously, people describe vivid colours, or colours they don't recognise from earth. Some say the light there is very bright but doesn't blind their eyes. Many people see green open spaces in heaven, meadows or places with lots of lakes, rivers, trees and flowers. Many describe parks or spending time by water (a beach, river or lake). Water appears to have life and a consciousness to it, and flowers and plants do, too. Everything seems full of vitality.

Some describe a multitude of animal life, including species that don't normally interact safely on this side of life. When they don't need to eat other creatures to survive, animals of different varieties can connect (a lion and a lamb, maybe?).

Life seems to exist at a more leisurely pace, although this is an illusion of sorts, because time does not exist as we know it. There is no such thing as past and future, with everything happening now in this current moment.

Some people have seen 'buildings' or structures on the other side, which appear to be created out of crystal; others have seen places they call 'Halls of Learning' or 'Halls of Teaching'. There are numerous gathering places, or spaces, where people (spirits) get together for fun or to listen to teachings by more advanced spirits. Sometimes buildings appear to have no roof. Although steps are seen, people glide up them rather than walk and also float along corridors.

People have described how they think of a person or location and then instantly appear with that person or at that place. Buildings are described as being beautiful or majestic, and may be placed around a central courtyard with architectural features including fountains, pots of flowers or statues. The buildings look the same as the most beautiful of our own, but clean and in amazing colour combinations! They, too, may appear to glow or vibrate with energy. No one has ever described a sun in heaven, yet many talk of the warm, glowing light that exists all around. There seems to be no day and night, just an ever-present now.

Dolores Cannon, who is known for her conversations with people in the deepest levels of trance, recorded a fascinating dialogue in her book *Between Death and Life: Conversations with a Spirit*. Under hypnosis her client describes the afterlife and at one point is walking down a corridor with walls that look like they are made of the blue-and-gold crystal lapis lazuli and marble. This heavenly healing temple is described as like being inside a jewel box with opals and other semi-precious stones set into the walls.

It's all pretty fascinating, isn't it? Okay, let's examine some of these real-life experiences of death and dying in more detail. You'll recognise some of the features described in this chapter appearing in some of the true-life stories coming up.

Chapter 3

Visits from the Afterlife

Kathy wrote to me to share a 'warning' dream she had, which means she was visited by spirits who let her know what was to come. Her boyfriend was seventeen years old when he first suffered a heart attack, so even then Kathy felt that he might not live to a ripe old age. They hadn't spoken for a few weeks because of a falling-out about his lifestyle – Kathy says she constantly worried about him – and one night when she was sleeping she had a very realistic dream. Three people appeared to talk to her: her boyfriend's older sister, a man whom she describes as having the face of God as depicted by Western tradition and a woman she believed to be the Virgin Mary!

The spirits spoke to her and said that they would be coming to collect her boyfriend very soon. Kathy said she immediately objected, but they warned her that she must prepare herself and not worry because after he died he'd be with them.

Afterwards Kathy says she didn't take much notice of the dream, but tragically, a couple of weeks later, her boyfriend was found dead in his flat.

I know some people find these dreams helpful, especially young children when older relatives pass over, but I'm not sure I would want to know about every relative who was going to die ahead of time!

Marion's husband Russell visited just six days after his funeral. She'd gone to bed at about 11 p.m., and after reading for a while she turned off the light and went to sleep. At about 3 a.m. (she checked afterwards) she woke with a start to see Russell standing next to the bed on his side. Marion was startled but not scared and said, 'Hi, Daddio, how are you?' He didn't reply, he just looked at her. Because she had woken suddenly, her eyes were still tired, even though she tried to keep them open. As she blinked he was gone.

Then, in another dream experience, she found herself in a park near a beach, across the road from a bus stop. 'We had to catch the bus home,' she told me. 'He was sitting in the park with a number of his relatives who had already passed over: his sister, father, ex-wife and niece as well as two others.' Marion didn't recognise the other two people. They were sitting in a circle on the grass, talking; only Russell was facing her. She remembers calling out to him to hurry because the bus was due and she was worried they would miss it if he didn't run over. Then the other spirits all turned and looked at her, too. Because he didn't move, Marion started walking towards him, but no matter how many steps she took, the distance always remained the same. Then she woke up.

You might recognise the 'bus stop', which indicates that Marion (and maybe her late husband) had travelled to visit this mutual space – a journey. They were near a beach, a natural place that is common in these experiences. Although there doesn't appear to be a clear boundary in the story (no gate or doorway), Marion was unable to reach the part of the park that her late husband was in. He was clearly on his side of the invisible divide, with the other spirits who had passed on, and she was on her own side. No matter how hard she tried, she was not able to go 'all the way' to heaven.

Dorothy's friend Judy also came to say goodbye. Judy had been sick for some time when the visit came one Christmas. Dorothy was in church with other friends when something happened. She was singing when her eyes were drawn to the top of the Christmas tree. She says the star on the top seemed to glow white, and it was as if she felt her friend Judy listening and enjoying the music so strongly that an image of her formed clearly in her mind; Dorothy says it felt as if her friend was sitting in front of her.

The feeling was so intense that even though they were in the middle of a song she grabbed her phone and ran outside. As she looked at the phone she realised she'd missed a call from Judy's husband just ten seconds before. She rang back immediately and was stunned to discover he'd been ringing to let her know that her friend had passed away.

So many mutual friends of theirs were in the service that Dorothy scribbled a note to the pastor, who then announced the sad news to a stunned congregation. Dorothy felt that her friend might even have chosen that exact time of her passing, knowing all her friends would be together. Afterwards everyone stood around talking, sharing loving memories and their gratitude at having had Judy in their lives. Dorothy says that although she can't find words to describe the feeling, her friends all agree that they sensed Judy with them that day.

The timing of Judy's passing does seem rather strange, doesn't it? I've known several people pass on with 'good timing', including my own father. Forgive me, I'm not making light of the subject; however, in my own family the timing was certainly helpful. Dad died after he and Mum had sold their bungalow and just before they were due to move into their new large apartment. It meant that Mum was able to quickly alter her plans and move to a smaller apartment, which was more suitable for a single woman. If Dad had died just three weeks later, Mum would have been tied to an apartment she couldn't afford. The soul doesn't choose the timing exactly, but there is often a little flexibility.

Lainey's visit from her mum was an unusual one, in that her mum didn't seem to be aware at first that she had died. This can happen occasionally, but there is always an angel or guide waiting patiently nearby, ready to assist. Luckily in this case Lainey herself saved the day. Let me start her story from the beginning.

Lainey's mum died unexpectedly back in 2007. She was only fifty-two years old. As long as Lainey could remember, her mum had been dependant on alcohol. One Sunday morning she was doing a little bit of shopping for her mum; she'd wanted some bottled water and prepared fruit to help ease a sore throat, and Lainey popped it round to the house. She kept knocking on the door but there was no answer. She even tried ringing the phone, but her mum didn't pick up.

The daughter was standing looking at the window but couldn't see through it because the blinds were closed. She kept thinking, 'I wonder if Mum has fallen asleep on her good ear and has her deaf ear to the world.' Lainey considered if maybe her mum had been up late watching re-runs of the soaps she loved so much and was now catching up on her sleep. Then she said she became aware of a voice in her head. It kept repeating over and over: 'I'm here. I can see you at the door but I can't let you in … And I hear you ringing the phone but I can't answer it.' This random thought kept going through her mind, over and over, but it was only a few weeks later that she realised the significance of the voice.

Lainey says that at the time she had her husband and two daughters in the car waiting, so she decided the best option was to take the shopping home and phone her nan to ask if she'd heard from her mum. As it happened her nan had been trying to get hold of Lainey's mum on the phone all morning, and in the end it was decided that Lainey's husband would go with her nan back to her mum's to see if everything was okay. Sadly, when they broke in, they found that Lainey's mum had died in the living room.

The family were shocked, but clearly so was Lainey's mum. 'It was about three or four nights later that I had the strangest dream,' Lainey explained. In the dream Lainey was sitting with mum in her kitchen at her old table and corner bench. Her mum was asking her what was going on and she seemed genuinely confused about it. At this point her mum noticed other spirits sat with them in the kitchen, although she didn't recognise them. Lainey says she found herself explaining to her mum that she had passed over, that she had died in the early hours of the morning and was now a spirit. Her mum had difficulty accepting this at first and wondered how this could have happened without her knowing. How could she have died when her daughter was sat in the room with her, talking? Why was Lainey there herself? I can understand why the poor woman was bewildered at this point, but her daughter's words seemed to have a calming effect on her.

The following night Lainey had a second dream about her mother. This time they were sat in her living room; her mum seemed ready to leave but was concerned that the neighbours might see her, so she asked her daughter to check out of the window to make sure the coast was clear. Isn't that funny? Bless her! She didn't want the neighbours to see that she had died!

Lainey says she felt privileged to have had these dream visits from her mum. It seems clear that her part in the experience helped her mum to cross comfortably to the afterlife. It's not something we should ever worry about, though. Eventually she would have realised. Other spirits had already gathered around the woman and between them they would have helped her to realise gently that her time had come. No one is ever abandoned. Lainey did say that she found the experience a good one. After her mother's sudden departure she felt that the visitation meant she was able to say goodbye.

Saying goodbye is an important reason for these spirit contacts. It's not always possible to be with those we love as they pass over, and the dream contact (or in some cases the waking connection) brings much-needed closure to the living. As we've already seen, it may also have an important connection for the deceased, especially if, for example, they don't yet realise they have died.

Mandy had a very real dream in which her family were back in their old house. She and her mother were visiting her great-nan in her nursing home. Mandy recalls that her nan seemed happy and was smiling. Although it seems strange for these experiences to also include living relatives, it is fairly common. I've had a lot of visitation dreams like this myself. My late father will turn up in dreams where the family has gathered. I find myself looking around at everyone who is still alive and then suddenly noticing that Dad is sitting in an armchair. It's at this point that I become very lucid and will say to him, 'Hey, what are you doing here?' I completely realise that he has died. Dad usually jumps up with a big grin on his face and disappears, almost as if he has been caught doing something naughty! The experiences are not in the least scary, and are actually rather comforting and fun. Dad regularly pops in to keep an eye on things and doesn't just save his visits for when there is a problem. I'm assuming he finds himself with some spare time (heavenly time) and just whizzes over to check things out.

Here is another goodbye dream. Charlotte's great-nan had passed away on Christmas Eve. As the family were gathering up her things at her home, a neighbour knocked on the door. Charlotte answered and it was a young lady in her early twenties; she looked worried. The woman said she'd had a strange dream the night before and went on to explain it to Charlotte. There was a flash of light, and then a few figures started to become clear. In her dream the woman witnessed the sad family all huddled around as the older woman waved goodbye, telling them that she would be okay and would continue to watch over them forever and ever.

The time of the dream had been three in the morning – the exact moment when Charlotte's great-nan had left her body for her journey to the afterlife. I believe this 'dream' was a real soul connection in the early hours. In this case the family had not been aware of the visit, so, unable to contact those she loved consciously, it seems Charlotte's great-nan had cleverly found someone who was able to share it with them. In a way this is sometimes better. It's easy to write off our own experiences as just a dream, but this young neighbour had no reason to come round and lie to people she didn't know or share a normal dream (in fact, she was taking a bit of a chance; it's possible that the family could have been offended by the message, so it was quite a gift to them that she put embarrassment to one side to do this).

This next story is very unusual. Sally wrote to say that she was getting married and had a strong urge to change the date of her wedding, so she went along with it and brought the date forward. Sadly, on the day, her father was unwell and couldn't attend the wedding, which Sally was very disappointed about.

Around the same time some friends had made a booking to see a medium. Before the appointment came through, Sally's dad was taken seriously ill. Sally still went to the medium and was the first of the group to chat to the woman that evening. The medium brought through several relatives from the afterlife, but then Sally was confused. The medium had her father with her and he was bringing a message. Her dad was still alive at the time, so she was shocked! Through this woman he told her the message: 'I am here to prepare you for the inevitable, but I will always be with you.' Sally said she knew it was her dad, and strangely the medium even mimicked some of his physical habits as she spoke.

Sally spoke to her sister about the reading and the following day they went to visit their father. He had taken to his bed and before Sally left she told him that she loved him and that she would visit the next day – words she always used. Her dad always used to say, 'See you tomorrow, love you,' but this time he answered, 'Goodbye, Sal, I love you.'

After the visit, Sally and her sister sat in the car and both cried and hugged each other, knowing their father probably didn't have many days left. Tragically, just eight minutes later their step-mum rang to tell them that their father had just passed away peacefully. Sally and her sister were shocked, but right away Sally realised that the following day was her original wedding day. It would have been even harder to get married the day after her father had passed, so the fact that she had brought the date forward now seemed more than a coincidence. Likewise, her dad's change of wording on their last visit may have indicated that his spirit, at least, had some indication that his time was near.

Although this story doesn't really have a happy ending as such, the paranormal circumstances surrounding this passing do seem to indicate that a spirit intervened somehow. And like the story before it, even though the dad himself was not consciously aware that his time was extremely near (as far as we know), his spirit certainly knew.

Mike's dad also passed during the holiday season; Christmas Day, to be exact. Mike told me that after the death, his mother, sister and brother all had dreams in which his dad appeared to them, but he didn't. At the time of his dad's passing, Mike admitted he'd been going through some difficult personal problems and that his dad, when living, had no knowledge of this.

He didn't really think any more about this until two or three years later. Mike thought he'd moved on, but clearly his dad had other ideas. He finally appeared in a dream visitation to Mike and seemed disappointed about the way Mike had lived his life previously – in his new heavenly state, Mike's past had been revealed to him, which meant Mike was now able to speak to his dad about it face to face. He apologised to his dad about the mistakes he'd made in his life. His dad seemed satisfied with this and told his son that he was going to fix things for him. I've had this type of thing come up in dream visits before, where our deceased loved ones occasionally have the opportunity to make little changes in our lives (usually, though, the deceased are only permitted to help out if their own passing was premature; they passed earlier than they were meant to and, had they been alive, they would have been able to help us).

Mike says he has no idea if his father had been given permission to put right mistakes or not, but what he did say was that he is now in a new relationship, with two wonderful stepchildren who see him as a dad rather than a stepdad. He's happy in his life and doesn't feel so guilty about his past any more. I'm not sure that our deceased loved ones can fix all of our problems, or even some of them, but it's nice to think that every now and again they might be able to help out just a little bit.

When Kim's father passed away suddenly the event was made even more traumatic as both she and her mother had vivid dreams in which her father told them he was not ready to die. This can happen occasionally when the soul feels they have missed something they needed to do, or, as we have already seen, they didn't get to say goodbye to loved ones.

Kim was upset to think that her dad was sad he was dead.

About two weeks after her dad's funeral Kim went to bed and, as usual in the weeks following his passing, she struggled to fall asleep. While she was lying there with her eyes shut (although she was very much awake), she saw a vision of her dad standing by the door, looking young and healthy. He finally seemed happy and in her head she heard him say, 'I am fine now, it's okay.' Then he walked to the door. The door opened and behind it was a brilliant white light that filled the room. He looked back at his daughter and smiled before walking into the beautiful light beyond. The door shut behind him.

Kim sat up in bed and was stunned to see the dazzling light still shining around the edge of the door in her room. She told me it was a life-changing moment for her; not only did it confirm that there was an afterlife, but it also took away the great sadness she and mum were carrying. I'm so glad her dad was happy to move on to the next stage of his soul's life and that he was able to come back one last time to let his daughter know he was okay. I'm sure it was an extra burden they didn't need during their time of grieving.

Chapter 4

Visiting Heaven

Where dream visits from those on the other side are fairly common – even the ones where we seem to meet them in some sort of middle realms or waiting area – having the opportunity to visit the afterlife when you haven't died is much rarer. It's a privilege and a very special prospect. When my uncle visited me from the afterlife once, I asked if I could go and visit heaven, but I was told no, not until I died. Nevertheless, some people have had this experience without going through death or near death.

Let me share Sandra's tragic story with you. She was left devastated when her son and his partner 'crossed themselves' over to the other side. The two men had desperately wanted children of their own and she felt this might have contributed to their decision. In her experience she seems to have visited the two men, even though they didn't speak to her directly.

Sandra told me that she had read most of my books. One was given to her by her daughter, who thought my true-life tales would be comforting; they were. Sandra rang her mother to tell her about the book, and her mum said she also had a book for her to read, which, strangely, turned out to be another of my books. Both women felt that the spirit world had been involved in this coincidence.

After her son's death, Sandra had four very vivid dreams, and she says she can still remember them like they were yesterday. Each of the dreams is like a snapshot of a story. Just as she was dropping back to sleep one morning, the first experience happened. 'My son was in my house,' she says. 'I opened my bathroom door and he was crying on his mobile phone.' Then in the second dream Sandra found herself in a haunted house. In the background she heard a familiar song, the one that had been playing at her son's funeral. In the third dream, her son was moving out of his old flat and his partner was with him. Then finally, in the fourth dream, her son was with his partner again and this time they had the baby they had wanted so badly on earth. Sandra says that these dreams brought her comfort, knowing they were finally at peace.

Janet had her experience shortly after her boyfriend's mum had died. She told me that she had been sitting on her bed praying and sending out healing prayers for both her boyfriend and his father. They were very upset at their sudden and unexpected loss when – and this is where it gets weird,

Janet said – she 'felt' herself being 'yanked' out of her body sideways.

Janet found herself in the most beautiful garden. She was overwhelmed by what she could see and found it hard to describe the place where she now found herself. Janet did try, though. These were her words: '… the colours, the music, the light … I knew where I was and wondered how I had done it. Then came what I can only describe as a column of light. I "knew" that this "light shape" was my boyfriend's mum.'

The recently departed woman was now this light. She had an important message for her son (which Janet asked to remain private), but once the message had been passed on, the woman faded away and Janet says she sort of 'jumped' back into her body again. Afterwards, Janet sat and cried for ages – even after all this time she says she still cries when she thinks of the heavenly place she visited that day. 'When I think of the beauty of the other side,' she explained, 'I simply cannot describe it. It brings a lump to my throat and tears to my eyes.'

When her own mum lay dying some time later, she was grateful to be able to share with her the beauty that she'd seen that day, and that her mum would be able to meet up with her parents once more. Janet is lucky enough to have seen heaven in the way that normally only those who have a near-death experience do (and, one assumes, those who get to stay do, too). I know that many people would volunteer to have a similar encounter if they could do so safely. I wonder, with medical science changing all the time, if this might one day be possible. I believe it would not only take away the fear of death, but it would also help us to enjoy our short lives on this planet all the more, too.

This wasn't Janet's only experience, though, as she recalls a visit from heaven when she was a little girl, too. She told me that when her grandpa was dying she saw her deceased nana standing at the end of his bed. 'I knew I wouldn't see him again after that day,' she confided, 'and I was right – he died during the night.' As we know from the previous chapter, her nana had come to escort her grandpa home.

Diane wrote to tell me about her experience. She explained that after she lost her godfather she found herself standing on some stairs that had a light at the top of them. It was a beautiful light and when she reached the top she saw very high walls on either side of an opening. A little further into the scene she noticed a lower wall, and this one she was able to see over. Diane was stunned to see beautiful crisp green grass; the fields and trees went on for miles.

While she was drawn by this breathtaking view she suddenly spotted her godfather, Uncle Ronnie, appear around the corner of the tall wall. He was wearing shorts and looked a picture of pure health.

He smiled and said hello, and immediately she recognised his voice and replied, 'Uncle Ronnie, is that you?' He told her he wanted her to do him a favour. He asked her to let his wife Betty know that he was okay and to ask her to 'stop going to that spiritualist' to make contact with him! He said he would visit personally when he could see she was ready to understand. I personally found this comment very useful; it might even answer the question many people have, which is: 'Why doesn't my loved one come to visit me from the other side?' We may feel ready, but perhaps, after all, we aren't.

Diane said she would pass on the message, but at the same time she was intrigued by the heavenly scene in front of her. She asked him what it was like to live in heaven and Ronnie said, 'I love it, I am home.' He apologised that he'd had to leave (die), and sympathised that it was such a shock for the family. He seemed keen for the family to stop crying and wanted them to know that he was at peace and was well now. He kindly reminded her that he would be there to meet each family member when their time came, to help escort them to the afterlife. Ronnie wanted his family to know that heaven was a beautiful place and that there was nothing to be scared of.

Diane asked if she would be permitted to go into the fields and have a look around, but her godfather refused. He stressed how important it was for her to take care of her health and warned her (unusually) that she, too, would face a setback in the future but that he was not permitted to share any further details. His final words were that he loved her.

She was so moved by the experience that she woke up crying; she was under no illusions that it had been completely real and passed on her godfather's message as promised. Incidentally, the 'setback', she tells me, was that a while later she had a stroke. I'm pleased to say that Diane recovered fully after her health scare and is now well enough to go about her usual business.

From my own experience I know that our deceased loved ones don't normally discuss our illnesses with us, unless they are given special 'permission' from the other side. From other stories people have shared, we learn that our illnesses and accidents normally form part of the soul growth we have chosen. By dealing with these things our soul grows and develops. Strange as this may seem, I've been told on numerous occasions that we chose these experiences before we were born. If you are interested in finding out more information about why and how this works, I would recommend the bestselling book *Journey of Souls* by Dr Michael Newton.

I received an email from Angela some while ago now; she was kind enough to let me know that my books helped her after her father passed on. From my own experience and those of my readers, I realise that paranormal encounters after the loss of a loved one are very common. What is hard is knowing what to do with them or how to comprehend what has happened. I know it helps a lot to read a book full of similar stories from others – this is the basis of most of my books! Once you've read that you are no longer alone you immediately feel better about what has happened to you.

Angela explained to me how lots of strange things happened after her dad passed. She explained how the lights would come on when no one was in the room and songs kept coming on the radio that reminded her of her dad when she'd been thinking of him. One day, she and her mum were talking about Angela's dad and they heard a loud crashing sound coming from the kitchen. They both rushed in and found three kitchen utensils lying on the floor. They had fallen in a strange way. Angela sent me a photograph and they were all in a line, equally spaced out, as if they had been placed that way. At the time they both wondered if maybe this had been a sign from Angela's dad.

Every night Angela asked her dad to appear in a dream and give her one last hug. Eventually she was rewarded. The day before what would have been her dad's birthday, she finally had a visitation experience while she slept. Angela found herself walking down a high street, and when she turned around she saw her dad coming out of a shop. He smiled and said to her, 'I haven't got long, I'm not supposed to be here.' His daughter responded by repeating her original request of wanting a goodbye cuddle. Her dad held out his arms, and the experience was so real she was able to smell his aftershave and feel his rough face, and even when she woke up she could still feel his arms around her for a few moments. Angela was ready the following day to scatter her dad's ashes with her family.

This time the heaven/earth boundary wasn't apparent, but no doubt it was there, perhaps in one of the shops or the shop doorway itself. I remember hugging my own dad in dreams after he passed over, and my sisters have been lucky enough to have the same experience, even dancing with him on occasion. For us, too, the encounter was completely real. I remember holding my dad's hand and as I woke I could still feel his hand in mine. Magic!

Here is the perfect story to end the book. Luciana wrote to me some while ago – she had a mystery heavenly visit. She told me that back in 2003 she became pregnant but was devastated when her boyfriend left her shortly afterwards. Luciana found herself crying all the time.

One night, when she finally got to sleep, she had the most real and vivid dream. A woman appeared to her – someone she didn't recognise but she recalls that the woman had on a white dress. The woman handed over two babies in the dream – they were both so different: one had blond hair and the other brown hair. The woman spoke to Luciana and said, 'Don't be sad, these are your babies. God sent them for you.' Luciana was shocked. Two babies? The woman in white continued: 'Take care of your twin babies!'

Even though she was stunned at the message, she also recalls more detail. It was the most vivid experience, she said to me. 'I know when a dream is just a dream, but this was so much more!' Then she went on to describe what else she saw, including a big river in a breathtaking setting – it was a 'sunny day', with beautiful light. It reminded me so much of the other heavenly visits I've heard about.

In the morning, Luciana went to the doctor. The heavenly woman in white was right; she was having two babies. Although at first concerned about the work of two, as they always say, double trouble, double the fun! And yes, I'm pleased to report that Luciana went on to have healthy twins, just as the spirit had 'warned' her. ☺

And so we're left with a big question. Do we choose to believe that life ends after the human body passes on, or do we consider all the thousands (possibly millions) of experiences that people have shared and wonder if, yes, life continues after physical death, just in a different form to what we are familiar with?

Touching Heaven

I've been researching this phenomenon for many years now and shared some of my favourite real-life stories with you in numerous books (piles of them!). I never tire of hearing about these magical encounters, and I know that many of my readers feel the same way. If you've had a paranormal experience of your own then I'd love to hear from you. You can contact me through my website. If you're still unsure, or this has whetted your appetite and you want to know more, then I've many more books of true-life accounts for you to enjoy.

Thank you for reading and I look forward to connecting with you again in the future.

Best wishes,
Jacky Newcomb
'The Angel Lady' x

www.JackyNewcomb.com

Moving Memoirs

Stories of hope, courage and the power of love…

If you loved this book, then you will love our
Moving Memoirs eNewsletter

Sign up to…

- Be the first to hear about new books

- Get sneak previews from your favourite authors

- Read exclusive interviews

- Be entered into our monthly prize draw to win one
  of our latest releases before it's even hit the shops!

Sign up at

www.moving-memoirs.com